30 Days to Eliminate Clutter and Debt

30 Days to Eliminate Clutter and Debt

Your Inner Guide to Order and Financial Security

Paula Langguth Ryan
and Janet L. Hall

Published 2024 by Gildan Media LLC
aka G&D Media
www.GandDmedia.com

30 DAYS TO ELIMINATE CLUTTER AND DEBT. Copyright © 2024 by Paula Langguth Ryan. All rights reserved.

No part of this book may be used, reproduced or transmitted in any manner whatsoever, by any means (electronic, photocopying, recording, or otherwise), without the prior written permission of the author, except in the case of brief quotations embodied in critical articles and reviews. No liability is assumed with respect to the use of the information contained within. Although every precaution has been taken, the author and publisher assume no liability for errors or omissions. Neither is any liability assumed for damages resulting from the use of the information contained herein.

Front cover design by David Rheinhardt of Pyrographx

Interior design by Meghan Day Healey of Story Horse, LLC

Library of Congress Cataloging-in-Publication Data is available upon request

ISBN: 978-1-7225-0692-6

10 9 8 7 6 5 4 3 2 1

For Mary Lee

Contents

How to Use This Book 9

1 Focus on What You Want 13
2 Quench Your Thirst for Silence 17
3 Cultivate Courage 21
4 Embrace What You've Made Unimportant 27
5 Plan to Succeed 31
6 Joyfully Embrace (or Turn Down) Gifts 35
7 Just Be 39
8 Release Attachment to Outdated Beliefs 45
9 Embrace Playtime 49
10 Toss Expected Outcomes 53
11 Bless Bills and Clutter with Gratitude 57
12 Go First-Class 61
13 Let the Universe Provide 65

14	Just Say No	69
15	Eliminate Prickly Attitudes	73
16	Accept (and Ask for) Forgiveness	77
17	Release Fear of What Might Happen	81
18	Pause Procrastination	87
19	Embrace Your Worthiness	93
20	Accept More Simplicity and Abundance	97
21	Appreciate Your Current View	101
22	Know Perfect Harmony Is Your Life	105
23	Acknowledge Your True Value	111
24	Take Nourishment from Everyone and Everything	115
25	Approach Life with Open Arms	119
26	Call on Your Inner Power	123
27	Nurture Your Discomfort Zone	127
28	Forgive All Past Decisions	131
29	Adopt a Positive Attitude	135
30	See Mountains as Speed Bumps	139
	Lather, Rinse, Repeat	143
	The TEASER	145
	DebtBuster Strategy	147
	Super DebtBuster Strategy	151
	Acknowledgments	155
	About the Authors	157

How to Use This Book

The last thing you need or want is another book with countless tips, tools, and strategies for getting rid of your clutter and your debt. Which is why we didn't write one. Instead, we pooled our combined fifty years of expertise in organizational psychology and transformational conflict management to bring you what you really want: the book to transform the beliefs, self-sabotaging go-to coping mechanisms, and deeply ingrained patterns that keep you stuck in disorder and financial chaos.

Which came first, the clutter or the debt? Doesn't matter. The two are joined at the hip. Completely codependent. In cahoots, pulling you into their downward spiral until you uncover, grab hold, and pull out the root causes that feed them.

By tackling clutter and debt together, you'll be empowering yourself to break these (seemingly) never-ending cycles. For good. You'll increase your peace of mind, concentration, self-worth, net worth, and confidence. You'll create order and financial stability. And you'll find yourself empowered to move boldly forward toward eliminating clutter and debt, because you're no longer held back by your fears and old stories and beliefs.

We intentionally made this book short and sweet. We recommend a one-a-day approach to each of the thirty chapters. Each chapter gives you a concrete inner action to take, examples from our own lives and work, navel-gazing questions to ponder, and tools for self-reflection. We wrap up each chapter with a daily call to action so you can practice these changes—and begin to see outer results in your clutter and debt as a result.

Travel through the journey at your own pace. Stick with one chapter for a few days, skip a chapter that seems too scary or annoying, keep coming back, even if you stop reading for a while. As you do this transformational inner work, you'll find yourself more intentional in your use of your space and possessions and how you manage your finances. Your motivation will come from more authentic and confident choices. Lasting choices. Mostly.

We know life is messy. Which means sometimes clutter and debt will return for guest appearances from time to time. The outer situation may appear familiar, but the way you view and react to this new (temporary) clutter and debt will be completely different.

Janet taught Paula many wonderful skills for organizing her life. An ordered life gave Paula room to play in the chaos of her mind as a writer. Whenever Paula returned home from a trip, her space would be filled with suitcases and boxes. Paula would unpack everything immediately, putting everything where she'd easily find it again.

Paula, in turn, taught Janet financial confidence. This confidence made it easy for Janet to navigate and negotiate large expenses into manageable payments so she wouldn't have to tap her savings or take on debt as she grew her business.

This book will help you do the same. If you are truly sick and tired of your clutter and debt, be sure to answer the questions in each chapter with rigorous honesty. Give yourself permission to experiment with the daily tasks we provide.

No matter the current state of your finances and clutter, this book arms you with lifetime skills that will transform how you view your journey toward the orderly, financially secure life you desire.

1

Focus on What You Want

*Success is focusing the full power of all you are
on what you have a burning desire to achieve.*
—Wilfred A. Peterson

As a child, what were you so committed to that you would do *anything* to accomplish your goal?

In the movie *Men of Honor*, Cuba Gooding, Jr. plays Carl Brashear, the son of a Kentucky sharecropper. Committed to becoming a Navy man, Brashear entered the Navy at age seventeen, the first year of desegregation. He soon discovered his true desire was to become a diver—but not just *any* diver. He wanted to achieve the highest rank any enlisted man could achieve: Master Diver. Though he faced formidable obstacles (including an amputated leg), Brashear stayed focused on what he *wanted*. He didn't let himself become distracted by anything he *didn't want*.

When was the last time you sat down and truly decided what you wanted? Most of us spend hours talking and thinking and complaining about what we *don't want* in our lives. We say things like, *I'm sick and tired of paying bills and being in debt*, or *I can't stand all the clutter and chaos in my life*, but we never get clear on what we *do* want.

Most of us go through our days just trying to get through the day. Like Rhino, the hamster character in the movie *Bolt*, we run in circles all day, accomplishing very little that moves our dreams forward. Not a dent in our clutter. Not a cent reduction in our debt or increase in our savings.

We declare we simply don't have enough time. But according to Australian time management expert Robyn Pearce, what we lack is *focus*, not time. Everyone has the same amount of time every day; it's how we *use* our time that makes a difference in the quality of our lives.

To achieve an orderly and financially solvent life, look at what you're *focusing on*. What you focus on is what you receive. Is your focus on the chaos of your clutter and debt or on creating the orderly and financially stable life you desire?

For twenty minutes today, turn a stinkeye on the chaos from your clutter and debt. Declare that you're not giving that chaos any more time or attention. Instead, focus all your attention and energy on envisioning what you truly want.

What will having financial stability and an orderly life feel like? What will it look like? What one small next step can you take to move your goal forward?

Write out your answers in ways that declare *specifically* where you will focus and where you will concentrate your energy. Ignore all obstacles, all distractions. Keep asking yourself, *what is the next right and perfect action for me to take to move forward toward my goal?* Postpone any desire to procrastinate, and ghost all ego thoughts.

By focusing on what you want, thoughts of obstacles, distractions and negative self-talk lose their power over you.

We want you to empower yourself, and information is power. Look at your *specific* top three clutter issues and *specific* top three debt or cash flow issues. Ask yourself, *what solution can I create that moves me forward?*

For example, Paula rented a fully furnished house to write for a year and found herself distracted by the chaos in the kitchen. Drawers and cabinets full of utensils she knew she'd never use, mixed in with a few usable items. Tackling the entire kitchen would have distracted her from her goal of writing daily. Instead, she focused on individual drawers or shelves. She grabbed three boxes. She put everything from a single drawer or shelf in one box. Whenever she needed a break from writing, she would set a timer for twenty minutes and sort items into two boxes: "keep" or "store." She repeated the process until the kitchen was set up to her liking, everything unneeded was stored away, *and* she had met her daily writing goal.

What information would help you create visible evidence that you're conquering your clutter and debt? For debt, it could be as simple as checking your account balances every day. Or using Paula's DebtBuster Strategy to create a list of all your debts, how much they are, their interest rates and your minimum payment and due date. For clutter, it could be using Janet's TEASER Sorting System. The TEASER helps you determine which action is best for each item: **T**oss, **E**nd, **A**ct on, **S**tore, **E**nter, or **R**efer-**R**ecycle-**R**ead-**R**epair. (You'll find versions of both at the back of this book and online at clutteranddebt.com).

Look for five items you can toss right now. Every action you take today toward what you want brings you closer toward the life you desire.

Affirm

Just for today, I focus on what I want.

2

Quench Your Thirst for Silence

Silence is the voice of the convinced; loudness is the voice of those who want to convince themselves.
—Dagobert Runes

Where, specifically, would you like more peace and quiet in your life?

Early in the Covid lockdown, when Paula sat on her front balcony with her family, she noticed something different. No traffic noises. No planes flying overhead. She whispered, "Hear that? It's so *quiet!*"

Most people have that same response when a herd of children leave the room or the last guests depart. Silence is supposedly the absence of sound. But as researchers at Johns Hopkins University discovered in 2023, silence really does have a sound. A sound that appeals to our desire for simplicity. For stillness.

Noise is all around us—and within us. Since outer noise is easier to pinpoint, today's focus is on the constant inner chatter that tells us we're not good enough, that we'll never get out of debt or get free from our clutter. The constant stream of consciousness that frets about misplacing important papers, the car keys, or an item you need to find right now. The voice that worries someone will pop by for a visit with the house looking like *this*. The inner chatter that berates us about looming bills, fearful of possible emergency expenses, wondering if today they will repossess the car.

Sometimes the constant worry tape plays loudly in our heads from the time we get up until the time we go to sleep. It may even permeate our dreams. Or we wear our debt and clutter like badges, boldly declaring excuses like, *my clutter keeps me creative* or *everybody has debt!*

Today, create space to transform the chaos of your mind with three steps:

1. **Immerse yourself in the silence.** Consciously spend twenty minutes doing something without talking, and without any added noise from electronics, media or other people. Remind yourself how refreshing silence can be.
2. **Stop talking about worries outwardly.** We say we want peace and quiet and freedom from our

clutter and debt. Yet we spend countless hours recounting our stressful problems: *I'll never get rid of this clutter or get out of debt. I'll always be broke. I'll never get ahead. I've always been disorganized and always will be.* Affirming these negative thoughts to ourselves or others (even through social media) strengthens what we don't want. It makes this negativity our reality.

3. **Speak only about positive changes you're making.** Talk about the steps you've taken to reduce debt and eliminate clutter. Congratulate yourself on your progress. Point out where you've made a dent in your clutter. Stop telling yourself and everyone else that "one of these days" you're going to get organized or be prosperous. Whenever a client told Janet they wanted to tackle their clutter and one day they'd "get around to it," she'd hand them a colorful cardboard circle emblazoned with "To It." Bypassing their excuses.

Whenever your brain tries to self-sabotage, create a simple incantation like, *chaos has no power in my life today* or *perfect order and financial stability are all I see in my life today.*

As our grandmothers used to tell us, if you can't say something nice about someone, don't say anything at all.

This also applies to what you say about yourself. Today, quench your thirst for silence by silently encouraging your progress and commitment.

Affirm

Just for today, I silently encourage my progress.

3

Cultivate Courage

You must give up your obsessive need for approval from people other than yourself.
—Terry Cole-Whittaker

Where do you seek approval from other people, especially when it comes to your clutter or debt?

Paula once had a young client who said he would take all the actions necessary to make different choices and create positive change in his life, *if* his ex would take him back *first*. He didn't have enough courage (or self-esteem) to change himself *for* himself.

If your desire to reduce clutter and debt is based on what other people want you to do, you're sabotaging yourself before you start. It's often been said you can't get sober for someone else. Lasting sobriety comes when it's what you desire *for yourself*—without any other motivation. The same goes for getting sober from clutter or debt.

Living from your *own* values and listening to your *own* inner positive voice will move you forward toward your goal of an orderly, financially secure life. Today, get clear on what you truly desire *for yourself.*

Janet's desire to get her affairs in order as her health waned brought her peace and joy as she relived precious memories and gave away pictures and other family heirlooms. Paula's desire to downsize allowed her to release possessions accumulated over the years.

Acting on what you desire may not seem easy. Let's not sugarcoat it: dealing with clutter and debt takes great courage. We hang on to things out of fear, and fear keeps us stuck.

While you want to eliminate the chaos in your life, the fear of losing your job or a catastrophic change may cause you to keep things you think you *might* need one day. Or you fear losing the time and money you paid for things. Or you think that giving away precious family heirlooms is courting death—or the wrath of family members.

You may want to break the debt cycle you're stuck in, but you're afraid to call your creditors to change a due date by a few days so you can reduce late fees. Or you're afraid to pay less than the minimum payment for fear of lowering your credit score. Or you're afraid to stop buying gifts for people because they'll think badly of you.

We all have things we *want* to do that we *don't* do—because we're afraid of the unknown. We fear being laughed at, ridiculed, humiliated, yelled at, put down, discounted, or judged. These fears keep us from having the orderly, financially secure life we desire.

Where are you afraid of how other people will react, will say no, or you either won't be heard or will be misunderstood?

Maybe you think you're not focused enough, or you lack the skills to talk with your creditors. Sometimes, we truly don't have the ability to take action on our own. More often, we simply don't know what *exactly* to say or do to create the change we want.

Where is that true for you? Where does taking action need to start with seeking advice? When Paula wrote Bounce Back from Bankruptcy, she included sample letters to creditors, with very specific language that readers could use to get a positive response. Having specific information reduced her readers' fears.

Janet always directed clients to write out scripts for fearful conversations they might have about what they were doing to reduce their clutter. She'd instruct clients to include possible responses or questions others might have and what their own positive response might be.

The courage required to conquer your fears already resides within you. Everyone has fears. Although we may not always eradicate those fears, we can press on until we get past them. Courage grows with every step we take outside our comfort zone.

That inner voice telling you to be afraid *isn't* your voice. So whose voice and values are you living by? What do you need to know? What information would make you feel more comfortable?

Today, cultivate courage. Give yourself permission to take one step outside your comfort zone with your finances. If you have a bill that's due on the first but is always late because you can't pay it until the seventh, call your creditor today. Explain when you get paid, how you are often late on paying them, and how you'd like to correct that by having your bill due date changed to a week later. You'll be amazed at how easily your creditors will work with you. They *prefer* to have your payment on time.

Do something similar with your clutter. Grab a box, bag, or container. Walk around your home and fill that box with things you see that you never use. If you're feeling courageous, drop off the box at a donation center.

If you need to build up your courage—or you're afraid you might need something in the box—seal it up, write a date on it that's six months from today, and stash the box. When the date arrives, toss or donate whatever's left in the box.

Affirm

Just for today, I make courageous choices.

4

Embrace What You've Made Unimportant

Argue for your limitations, and you get to keep them.
—Richard Bach

What's *really* important to you?

When Janet was diagnosed with liver cancer (which unfortunately turned out to be terminal), even though she planned on fighting and beating it, she wanted systems in place so everything was in order for her husband as she went through treatment and for the continuation of her life's work after she was gone. These two goals were really important to her.

To get crystal clear about what's really important to you, answer these seven questions:

1. What have you wanted to do for years that you still haven't done?
2. Why haven't you done it?

3. Where are you waiting until you have enough money or until you've cleared out enough space?
4. Where are you not wanting to rock the boat by following your dreams?
5. Where do you concentrate on helping others meet their goals instead of working toward your own?
6. Who relies on you too much for you to rely on yourself?
7. Where have you refused to even give yourself permission to have goals of your own?

Be radically honest with yourself as you answer these questions.

Armed with these answers, clearly declare what you want to do with your life. What debt do you most want to be free from? Be specific. What unused items do you want to get rid of? Again, be specific. You want a better life, right? So don't settle for the best you've ever had. The best you've ever had may only be a fraction of what you *can* have and be.

Embrace whatever you've made unimportant until today. Embrace and prioritize all the things that your heart desires but you've kept moving to the bottom of your to-do list. Still unsure of what your heart longs to do? Be rigorously honest and ask yourself:

Embrace What You've Made Unimportant

If I could do anything I want to do, regardless of what anyone else might say or think, regardless of where I might get the money to fund my dream or where I might learn the skills I want to learn, and if I knew I could not fail, what would I want to do, be, or experience?

Once you've got that answer firmly fixed in your mind, ask yourself:

How is my clutter or debt keeping me from achieving this goal?

Eliminate debt payments, and you free up the money to do what you dream of doing. Reduce clutter, and you free up space for a sideline business, a hobby, or a smaller, less expensive house.

Imagine you've just been offered a free home—real estate that matches your dreams—to use any way you like. The only catch is you must move within twenty-four hours. What would you absolutely take with you and what would you willingly release?

When Paula's family downsized, they decided to look at everything they didn't want to take with them. They decided they wanted their downsizing to be easy and effortless. They didn't want to invest time and energy listing things for sale or for free giveaways. Everything could either go in the dumpster or to a new home—to family, friends, neighbors, or the local thrift shop. They encouraged people to spread the word. Many things had been given to them, so they wanted to bless others by passing their belongings on. When moving day arrived, everything had been rehomed or left at the request of the new occupants.

Releasing items and beliefs that no longer serve you starts with clarity about what is important to *you*. Write down everything you can think of that is important to you. No matter how odd or ridiculous or far-fetched or obscure your choices seem, don't judge or filter what is important to you. Just write it down. When you are done, look over the list and select five things you want more than all others. Write these five items down, and put your list somewhere you can look at it every day.

Whenever you want to take an action, spend money, or bring something into your home, ask, *how is this bringing me closer to what's important to me?*

If it's not bringing you closer, take a pass on that unimportant desire. Stay focused on what *is* important to you, and you will effortlessly begin to accomplish your goals. There are no limits except the limits we set for ourselves.

Affirm

Just for today, I release everything that's no longer important to me.

5

Plan to Succeed

I cannot give you the formula for success, but I can give you the formula for failure: try to please everybody.
—HERBERT BAYARD SWOPE

Where is your belief about success and failure *truly* what you believe? And where is what you've come to believe based on your past experiences and other people's fears or expectations?

Janet turned forty in 1994. She decided she no longer wanted to commute two hours each way to her job in Washington, D.C. Full-time jobs were scarce in Southern Maryland, so she took on five part-time jobs—one of them being working for Paula, who had just started a publishing company. As Janet helped Paula grow her business, she was able to quit her other part-time jobs until she became a full-time employee. After three years of working with Paula and getting her organized,

Janet launched her organizing and time management company.

Janet created success in her life, using this concrete success plan:

I want to free up twenty hours a week that were previously spent commuting and create a meaningful life for myself in my community.

She started taking action to make that plan a reality without any attachment to *how* that plan would unfold or what other people would think. You can do the same!

Your definition of success is *yours*. Today, declare that you have a concrete success plan for creating an orderly and financially secure life. That's what you want, and what you want is *your* business. *How* the fulfillment of your plan comes to you is none of your business. Immerse yourself so deeply in what you want that you no longer notice anyone else's opinions or disappointments. Self-sabotage isn't even an option when you dedicate yourself to achieving your plan. Focus on honoring your desire for a clutter- and debt-free life.

Work your plan today with great zeal and determination. What that looks like is up to you, so long as you keep it simple and stay on task.

Just for today, you will choose to put everything you touch back where you found it (or where you could more easily find it). You will choose to not create any new clutter or take on any new debt today.

Get clear on your concrete idea of success by answering these three questions:

1. What do I truly want to do with my money and space?
2. What within me is holding me back from successfully becoming clutter- and debt-free?
3. What tiny steps can I take today toward overcoming these obstacles?

Use your answers to support and motivate yourself to make your plan a reality, without attachment to *how* that plan unfolds.

Affirm

Just for today, I give myself permission to succeed in creating my orderly, financially secure life.

6

Joyfully Embrace (or Turn Down) Gifts

A gift—be it a present, a kind word or a job done with care and love—explains itself! And, if receivin' it embarrasses you it's because your "thanks box" is warped.
—Alice Childress

Where do you consciously or unconsciously limit what people give you?

Our friend Judith, director of Scottsdale's Center for Expanding Consciousness, once invited us to lunch in the center's kitchen. Judith was talking to us about how the center was constantly needing paper goods. A few minutes later a center member popped into the kitchen and donated bags full of paper towels, paper cups, napkins, and toilet paper.

Without hesitating, Judith said, "Oh, you shouldn't have. Thank you." With those three simple words—"you shouldn't have"—Judith dismissed the request she had made for these items, which the universe had gladly fulfilled pretty much instantly.

Every time we turn down a gift—consciously or unconsciously—we limit ourselves from receiving all the universe has to offer us. Accepting a gift honors and empowers the giver *and* the receiver. Think about the crestfallen look on a child's face when you refuse a gift from them!

For twenty minutes, dive into why you impulsively reject gifts you want—and why you accept gifts that don't truly benefit you—by answering these five questions:

1. When in my life did I not joyfully receive gifts offered to me?
2. When do I turn down help regarding clutter or debt?
3. When don't I think I'm worthy or deserving of a gift?
4. When have I turned down help because I'm embarrassed?
5. When do I feel obligated by gifts—thinking I need to do something in return that I either don't want to do or don't feel worthy of doing?

You may be uncomfortable or embarrassed when people offer to pay for something or volunteer to help you with your clutter or debt. That discomfort may cause you to unconsciously refuse to receive the gift of their time and energy.

You may even justify your behavior by rationalizing that the gift being offered isn't *exactly* what you want. Some people are very uncomfortable receiving anything, whether it's a gift or an offer of help. Maybe you learned that you had to do everything all by yourself. Or past experiences taught you that receiving gifts meant something was expected of you in return, that a string was attached.

Old inner stories may tell you that you're not deserving of what's being offered. Doesn't matter. Today we leave the past in the past. The truth is, you *are* deserving! And it's time to learn to receive your true worth. It's time to see these things not as acts of charity or pity, but as gifts to be received with joy.

Today, notice your responses—your words, thoughts, and physical reactions—when people attempt to give you something or do something for you. When you're tempted to turn down a gift, first, ask yourself, *is this gift something that will help me meet my goals for an orderly and financially secure life?*

Triage the offer before accepting or declining. Quickly ask yourself: *will this gift add to my clutter or derail my efforts to declutter? Is this something I'll have to pay back or that will otherwise require me to add to my debt?* If either answer is yes, joyfully turn down the gift by saying, *I appreciate the offer AND I'm going to pass. Thank you.*

Chances are, an offered gift may simply make you uncomfortable because of your past thoughts about gifts. If the gift is triggering an old belief, ask the person one question, *are you sure this is a gift?* If the answer is yes, say. *thank you, I accept!*

Today, when someone wants to feed your spirit by giving you gifts that reduce your expenses or offering to roll up their sleeves and help you dig through your clutter, give yourself permission to joyfully receive.

Affirm

Just for today, I welcome all gifts with joy.

7

Just Be

Nothing really changes until we do.
—Dan Millman

Where are you investing time and money in actions which never seem to bring you closer to your goals of a clutter-free, debt-free life?

Paula once told a harried friend to "just be." The friend snapped back, "It's on my to-do list!" Sound familiar?

By day's end you're exhausted, with little or nothing to show for your efforts. All that time spent churning your wheels, trying to keep too many plates spinning on their little sticks each day. You feel behind before you even get out of bed; there's no time to appreciate the beauty around you, thank anyone, or even take a deep breath.

The playwright August Wilson once called the director of a play he was writing to say he couldn't finish the third act because he'd somehow written himself into a box. The director responded by telling Wilson, "You're the writer. You wrote yourself into the box—so write yourself out of it!" Wilson sat down and drew a picture of himself inside a box. Then he created a scene where he wrote himself out of the box, which gave his mind the quiet time and space to figure out a solution to the play's final act.

Today quiet your mind, be present, and become open to possible solutions. Think outside the box you've created for yourself.

When we're busy *doing*, it's easy to enmesh ourselves so deeply in a problem that we get out of sync and out of balance. We fill our time with quick fixes rather than permanently writing ourselves out of the box we've created.

Today you're going to do something radical: release your worries, problems, and expectations. In your mind, stop trying to keep the plates spinning. Stop thinking about all the actions you *must* take, and let all the plates crash to the ground. Give yourself twenty minutes of peace and quiet.

When time's up, ask yourself, *what one action can I do differently today with one of these spinning plates that would rewrite my story of being stuck in this cycle of "doing?"*

Taking action on your clutter can be as simple as picking a specific place to put items you commonly misplace. Ask yourself, *where will I find this?* Perhaps use a bowl or hook by the front door for keys and the contents of your pockets so you can always find your license or debit card.

Same goes for financial actions. Write billing due dates on your calendar (a few days before they're due!) so you stop incurring late payment fees, or simplify your savings by setting up an automatic sweep of $5 or more into your savings account.

Your action on a clutter or financial issue could even be more introspective, such as answering these three questions for yourself:

1. Where am I keeping a plate spinning because I'm afraid of what happens if I stop?
2. What do I think will happen if I let the plate fall?
3. If I don't have everything I need, how can I use what I *do* have to create what I want?

Your answers can lead you to actions that are both simple and scary.

A client of Paula's was stuck in a payday loan cycle where her entire weekly paycheck went to pay off the previous payday loan. Without enough money to get through the week, she repeatedly had to take out *another* payday loan. She didn't know how to stop the cycle. If she didn't have to repay the entire loan each week, she knew she could easily make ends meet, but the payday lender said they wouldn't take smaller payments.

Just because someone says you can't do something, doesn't mean it's true!

Paula suggested having the bank put a stop payment order on all future automatic withdrawals by the payday lender. With a new weekly budget, the client was able to meet her expenses *and* send the payday lender a weekly money order with a portion of what they were owed. With the stop payment order in place, the client wrote herself out of the box and eventually paid that last payday loan in full.

Stop spinning and give yourself clarity. Quiet your mind so you can see the bigger picture. When your fears recede, your mind has more room for different solutions. Solutions that create different results, immediately.

Today, practice this new action of doing nothing and simply be present. Sit and sip a cup of tea. Stare at something in nature. Wait patiently in lines or at stoplights without picking up your phone. When someone brings a problem to you, wait twenty minutes before responding, giving them time to find their own solution.

Practice pausing whenever you're tempted to spin yourself into another box. If you're looking to add something new to your daily to-do list, add, *just be*.

Affirm

Just for today, I let myself be still enough to think outside the box.

8

Release Attachment to Outdated Beliefs

*What the mind can conceive and believe,
the mind can achieve.*
—Napoleon Hill

Which beliefs hold you back from being everything you can be, and from doing everything you can do?

In the movie *Forrest Gump*, Tom Hanks plays a mentally challenged man who never believed he was limited. He didn't let fear, ignorance, old stories, or lack of vision keep him from achieving anything. He ran his own business, became a millionaire, had the girl of his dreams, and empowered others to overcome their outdated beliefs.

But that's a movie, right? That can't happen in real life, can it?

Paula went from being a throwaway teenager, on her own at seventeen, to achieving many of the same goals as Forrest Gump. Janet went from being a high-school dropout to earning her GED, creating her own business, and becoming a highly sought-after international speaker, organizer, time management consultant, and college instructor!

We *all* have the same potential for greatness within us. Most of us don't fully tap into our potential out of fear, ignorance, or old stories running amok in our brains. Simply put, we don't *believe* we can "get 'er done."

Old beliefs are so ingrained in us that it sometimes takes a bit of effort to ferret them out. Start by finishing this statement:

I want to _____ , *but I can't, because* _____ .

A wise person once said, "Everything after the word *but* is an excuse." Read your fill-in-the-blank statement again, starting with everything you wrote after the word *but*.

Your excuse may be something along these lines:

I don't have enough time.

Other people won't get rid of anything.

My creditors won't work with me.

I never have any money to pay down my debts.

Write fill-in-the-blank statements for every desire you have that you're not achieving. Armed with this list of excuses, you'll have a good idea of what you *truly* believe. Which in turn gives you a detailed roadmap for transforming those beliefs.

The Napoleon Hill Foundation shared this tidbit in its October 24, 2021 Thought for the Day: "You may not be able to achieve everything you'd like, but you won't accomplish anything unless you believe you can."

When you identify the culprit—the thought or excuse holding you back—you can transform it. To get started, you can replace the four excuses from earlier simply by replacing the word *but* with the word *and*, like this:

EXCUSE: *but* I don't have enough time.
NEW BELIEF: *and* I now have enough time to accomplish all that is mine to do today. If something doesn't get done, it wasn't mine to do today.

EXCUSE: *but* I'm afraid to get rid of things I might need.
NEW BELIEF: *and* I now look for other ways I can find the items or papers I might need, so I can release them from my home.

EXCUSE: *but* creditors won't work with me.
NEW BELIEF: *and* I now find creative ways to work with my creditors, regardless of what they say they will or won't do.

EXCUSE: *but* I never have any money to pay down my debts.

NEW BELIEF: *and* I now send a dollar every month toward a debt, knowing this action moves me closer to being debt-free.

Make a list of a few new beliefs to replace your old excuses. *See* the orderly and financially secure life you *are* achieving, one moment at a time. Write down the things you believe you *can* do—and then back up your beliefs with your words and actions.

Move away from outdated beliefs and excuses, and you'll subconsciously shift your energy toward what you want. Toss your old beliefs, lighten your mental load, and you'll clearly see more order and financial security in your life.

Affirm
Just for today, I embrace new beliefs that empower me.

9

Embrace Playtime

The creation of something new is not accomplished by the intellect, but by the play-instinct.
—Carl Jung

Where do you take life too seriously?

Often people are so mad at themselves for their clutter and debt that they banish themselves from anything even approaching fun.

Our daily stresses can make playtime more challenging. But play doesn't have to stop when we're grown up. Maybe you've forgotten how to have fun. If so, watch how children play. Children can make a game out of anything, even vacuuming, cleaning out the car, or wiping down kitchen walls. They only start to view what they're doing as a chore when we teach them it's a chore—the same way we've taught ourselves that managing our clutter and finances is a chore. A big, boring, tedious, scary chore.

The problem is, when you're not playing, you're not laughing; and laughter cures a lot of ills. Laughter can make clutter seem less daunting. Laughter can make bills seem less scary. Laughter can turn any chore into a game.

Growing up, Paula's family loved watching television together, and, as a family of six they also had a lot of evening chores. Here's how they did both. Each night, they would appoint one person to stand watch when commercial breaks started. Everyone else would spring into action, cleaning up, swapping laundry, doing other chores as needed. When the show was coming back on, the timekeeper shouted out, and everyone hurried back to relax and enjoy the show until the next round of commercials. Turning chore time into playtime.

Give yourself permission to play today. Invest twenty minutes incorporating playtime into the task you're doing. Who says you can't dance around the house while picking up and putting away clutter, or jam to uplifting music while you take care of your bills? Think outside the box and find the fun in what you're doing. Create an atmosphere of play while you're getting organized or making stronger financial choices. Or reward yourself in small playful ways each time you finish small tasks that move you closer to being clutter- and debt-free.

Our spirits and souls crave play; its positive energy feeds us. Embrace playtime as you create order and financial security. Set aside the time intentionally. Put it on your calendar as a clutter-crushing or debt-busting playdate. Sing your own made-up song, blast your favorite empowering music, or choreograph your own wild dance. Activating your play instinct will generate a slew of new ideas for speeding up your journey toward order and financial stability.

Affirm
Just for today, I play with wild abandon!

10

Toss Expected Outcomes

*Through unexpected incidents, the universe tries
to teach you something. Learn the lessons.*
—Chin-Ning Chu

What unrealized expectations in your life frustrate you the most?

Too often we're so focused on *how* we want something to turn out, we don't realize it when the actual outcome is something better.

For example, when the two of us authors toured together, we always expected a full house at our events. One evening we arrived at our venue, set up, and waited—and not a single person showed up. The entire event had been sold out, yet no one was there. Instead of getting frustrated about a wasted evening, we decided there must be a reason for skipping this event, even though we had no clue what that reason might be.

We affirmed that *only good can come from this*. We packed up, went out to an early dinner, and returned to our lodging. There an event had just started, led by an incredibly fascinating woman who taught both of us important things about ourselves.

Letting go of our expectation for that evening opened us up to even greater good.

Having an expectation of your progress with clutter and debt—planning in advance what you're going to do and how others will react—can create resentment and trigger old sabotaging behavior.

We obsess over the complicated steps we think are required, or we fear repeating our old patterns—so why should we bother?

Our negative expectations of ourselves are exhausting. Too often we talk ourselves right out of taking the action we wanted to take toward creating our orderly and financially stable life.

Truth is, greater good can (and often will) come from a different outcome than the one your ego has in mind. Pay attention to where fear keeps you from acting. Maybe you're saving money or a possession because *someday* you want to use it a certain way.

Janet was once given many yards of fabric, which she wanted to use "one day" to create clothes and gifts. She gave herself one year to take action on the fabric, or out the door it would go. When that date came, she took the remaining unused fabric to an adult care center to use in their arts and crafts program. Many of the residents' creations wound up being award-winning entries at that year's county fair. And by letting go of the fabric, Janet gained new space to expand her office.

Maybe you're avoiding action on a financial issue because of penalties you might incur. Paula had a client who put off renewing her expired driver's license for *years*. The client went online, looked up the penalties, and saw hundreds of dollars of late fees. Rather than becoming paralyzed by fear, the client took time to release her negative expectation and focused on an expectancy that *only good can come from this*. She confidently walked into the department of motor vehicles, presented her ancient license to the woman at the desk, and stated calmly and confidently, "I've come to renew my license."

The woman took a look at the expired license and commented, "It's been a while, hasn't it?"

The client calmly agreed it had.

The woman's fingers flew over the keyboard, then she looked up and said, "That will be $10, please." Within minutes, Paula's client had a brand-new driver's license without having to pay extra fees.

These types of wonderfully unexpected outcomes can be yours when you become willing to toss your *expected* outcomes and adopt a sense of positive *expectancy* instead. After all, we rarely know the best outcome for ourselves, so keeping an open mind will keep you moving forward.

Today, release your preconceived notions of the worst that could happen, and create an expectancy for yourself about the good that *can* happen. When something doesn't go the way you want, rather than getting frustrated, angry, or sad, simply pause your deflecting thoughts. Even when you can't see *how*, trust that the outcome you're experiencing is designed to show you something even better that's available for you.

For example, a creditor or lender could be very open and receptive to a request you make. Or that person could say no—which might move you into a healthier relationship with your money.

Today, stay focused on your expectancy that only good comes from everything. You'll be surprised what the Universe has in store for you when you do.

Affirm

Just for today, I release my expected outcomes and make room for something better.

11

Bless Bills and Clutter with Gratitude

Fear sees limits, while love sees possibilities.
—Louise Hay

What do you *dread* most about paying down debts and decluttering—and what do you *enjoy* most about it?

Our feelings about our bills and belongings reveal much about how we feel about life in general. When Paula was first an adult, she used to dread paying her bills. She worked hard for her money all week, and all she had to show for it was a pile of bills.

The stack of unopened creditor envelopes grew higher, and she was angry and afraid. She hated her bills, hated creditors, and hated herself for the financial situation she'd created. The more ungrateful she was, the harder it was to pay the bills—until she focused on the gifts hidden within her bills.

Today, do some recon around your house. Set a timer for ten minutes, walk around your home and observe all the negative emotions that come up when you look at where you've spent money and how you've cluttered up your life. Just observe the negative feelings that come up. When the timer goes off, take a deep breath, stretch, and reset the timer. This time, walk around and observe your home again with a filter of *gratitude*. Allow yourself to see everything you love and value. It could be comfortable furniture, a washer that doesn't leak, the orthodontics bill that fixed crooked teeth, a vet bill for your beloved pet, clothes that fit just right. Piles of magazines, books, or DVDs that entertained you or taught you skills. Give thanks and extend gratitude to everything you see. Refocus on everything you have and what your bills enable you to do.

The electric bill reminds us how fortunate we are to have modern ways to wash and dry our clothes, watch movies with our families, read at night, or earn money using our computers. The pile of mending, laundry, or ironing reminds us how fortunate we are to have clothes to wear. The doctor's bill or insurance premium reminds us how fortunate we are for today's medical advances, and so on.

Today, see your life only through this new lens of gratitude. Give thanks for all your expenses and possessions. Give thanks for both the fear and the positive possibilities everything represents.

As you pay whatever you can toward a debt and release an item of clutter, take time to bless them all. Bless the electric bill for providing you with light and running all your appliances. Bless your piles of toys, papers, books—everything you're sorting—for providing you and your family with hours of enjoyment, ideas, and entertainment. Bless the credit card bills for the purchases you made, the vacations you took, and the emergency expenses you were able to pay.

Your gratitude and your blessings transform the energy of the money and possessions you're releasing, permeating everything you are and do. Show the universe you are ready, willing, and able to release what no longer serves you, and you'll soon find you have abundant space for what *does* serve you now.

As you feel increasingly empowered about your bills and belongings, it becomes easier to sort through mail and clutter. You'll find yourself eager to open bills when they arrive, because they contain important information you want to know. It becomes second nature for everything in your life to have a place where you'll easily find it. You'll also find yourself guided to return things where they belong when you're done with them.

Right now, think about something you're grateful for that's related to a financial situation or item of clutter that weighs heavily on your mind. Then take the action you're guided to take, with your mind filled with the certainty that you're on the right track.

Affirm

Just for today, I choose to be grateful for all my bills and clutter.

12

Go First-Class

If you refuse to accept anything but the very best,
you will often get it.
—W. Somerset Maugham

What things in your life do you not truly enjoy or value?

Still-useful items that are chipped, cracked, torn, frayed, held together with duct tape or twine may subconsciously project the thought that you don't deserve the best. The truth is, you *do* deserve the best. And it's time to start treating yourself as a first-class individual who feels worthy and deserving.

Paula knew an immigrant who came to America with just two brand-new dress shirts. Every other day, he would wash and iron his two shirts, so he always looked and felt his best. He never complained about owning only two good shirts. Instead, he focused on how prosperous he felt wearing his best clothes every day.

Having a first-class mindset isn't about what you *have*. It's about how you *feel*. Today, start upgrading your outer world by first upgrading your inner world. When someone compliments you on something, don't dismiss them with *oh, this old thing?* or *they're not real*, or *I got it at a garage sale*. Instead, simply say *thank you*.

Release old thoughts and words you habitually use to devalue yourself daily. Ferret out items in your life that tie you to that lack mentality and release them. Start with nonessential items, like dishes and cups that are cracked or chipped, or clothes that are frayed, torn, or stained. Or things you can no longer use because they're broken or inoperable.

There is great truth in the saying "Out of sight, out of mind." When you eliminate these items from your sight, the lack they represent leaves your mind as well.

Instead of drinking out of an ordinary everyday glass, use your best glass or crystal for your morning juice. Dress first-class just for yourself, not because you're trying to make a good impression on someone else. Actions like these give you a different worldview *of yourself*, and they help others see you as you truly are.

People treat us the way we treat ourselves. Today, take time to treat yourself as you deserve to be treated. Release things in your life that are anything less than first-class, and begin using the finest things in your life every day.

Affirm

*Just for today, I choose to treat myself
to a first-class life.*

13

Let the Universe Provide

What you're looking for is already inside you.
—Anne Lamott

What are your go-to solutions to your debt and clutter problems? And where do you stand in the way of allowing the universe to provide *better* solutions for you?

Disappointment comes when we ask for what we want but aren't open to receiving it in the form in which it is delivered. For example, a few years ago, Paula's family had an unexpected large expense that they were paying off over time—and wanted to pay off faster. When her father-in-law passed away, Paula's spouse received a truck from his estate. A few months later, the truck was stolen and never recovered. The insurance company paid for the entire value of the truck, which was enough to pay off that unexpected expense.

It took time to shift from seeing the inherited (and stolen) truck as the loss of something precious to seeing it as having a different purpose—as the answer to the prayer to pay the outstanding bill in full.

Building up your trust in an absolute power—whatever name you give it—is easy, *and* it requires your focused attention. Deep within you, the solution resides. Today, get crystal clear on what you want by making three lists:

1. What I want to come into my life
2. What I want to leave my life
3. What I want to change in my life

Declare with complete conviction that you *know* the universe will move mountains to make your desires manifest in whatever form is best for you—as long as you focus on what you want and release all attachment to how your desires show up.

What you want is your business; *how* it comes to you is none of your business. It's not your job to come up with the solution; the universe will provide the outcome that is for your highest good, if you let it. All it takes is these three steps:

1. Know in your heart that the universe will provide for you.
2. Hold the thought that you *will* be guided to take each next action.

3. Release any worry or fear, and take action on the idea that comes to you, no matter how odd it seems.

The most random thought will often lead you to the right and perfect solution. Anytime you feel an urge to tell someone what you want, share it. Stay open to odd coincidences and unexpected events.

Maybe you're afraid to let go of something because you've had a loss in your life. Maybe you don't know how to ask for help with your clutter or debt, or you've asked before and you were disappointed when you didn't get what you wanted.

Today give yourself permission to let the universe provide you with the solution of how your clutter and debt will leave your life. Take action on the guidance you receive—immediately. Don't procrastinate your good away, and don't turn down the good that appears in unexpected forms. You've asked the universe for your good. Today, allow it to come to you.

Affirm

Just for today, I allow the universe to provide for me, and I take action on all guidance I receive.

14

Just Say No

The word NO is a complete sentence.
—Shonda Rhimes

Where in your life have you said yes to doing something you didn't really want to do?

For example, Janet kept working for Paula even when she decided she wanted to start an organizing business. Janet knew she'd miss having a steady paycheck. Paula would miss having Janet as a valuable member of her company. And they both would miss spending time together. But the publishing company was Paula's dream, not Janet's. So Janet bravely told Paula when she'd be leaving and why. Saying no to working on someone else's dream turned out to be a great move for both companies. In fact, a few years later, we were touring and writing together.

Saying yes when we really mean no is a complicated habit to unwind. Why do we do this to ourselves?

We say yes because we don't see another way forward. We say yes because we don't want to disappoint someone, or because we feel guilty when we say no. We want to be safe, liked, seen as generous. We don't want to hurt other people's feelings or be left out.

We say yes to friends who invite us out to dinner or who encourage us to add to our clutter, even though we're trying to save money and release things. We reach into our pockets to contribute when others ask for money for anything from a celebration to an emergency. We even say yes to—and keep—gifts we don't want instead of returning them or passing them along to someone who would love them.

Today, build the habit of saying no to what truly *does not* feed your soul.

Saying no to someone—risking their disappointment—may appear to be difficult. Especially if the request is important to another person. In truth, you're already a master at saying no. You say it to yourself all the time.

That's right: saying yes to others because it's uncomfortable to say no is your way of saying no to yourself and what you deem important. You abandon yourself, avoid being true to yourself, and stay stuck in the cycle of clutter and debt. But because you're reading this book, we assume that staying in debt and up to your eyeballs in clutter is not something every fiber of your being desires.

Too often, we willingly disappoint ourselves rather than someone else. In her poem "The Invitation," Oriah Mountain Dreamer wrote, "I want to know if you can disappoint another to be true to yourself."

Today, practice only taking actions that align with your personal truth. Today, take a step toward unlearning the habit of throwing your own priorities under the proverbial bus.

Let's start by following the advice of author Paulo Coelho: "When you say yes to others, make sure you're not saying no to yourself." Saying no to yourself teaches other people to say no to you. Saying yes to yourself teaches others to say yes to you. If you don't put yourself first, who will? You must be willing to be selfish in order to be true to yourself, to paraphrase "The Invitation."

Today, deliberately focus on saying yes to creating positive progress on your goals. Use any or all of these four strategies to develop the habit of saying no to others so you have room to say yes to yourself:

1. Today, take a deep breath and say no to at least one person who asks you to do something that will contribute to your clutter or your debt.

2. Say no to at least one request you don't feel positive about in your heart.
3. Say no to at least one request for your time and energy with a gentle, *that's not mine to do*. Then use that time and energy to free yourself from some clutter and debt today.
4. Pause before you say yes and say, *let me think about that*. Then take time to determine if your yes is a *yes* for both of you before you respond.

When people make vague requests like, "What are you doing Friday after work?" ask for clarification before you answer. The question may be a precursor to asking you to join them in an enjoyable activity, or it may be a way of hooking you into running an errand for them or joining them in a spending spree.

Affirm

Just for today, I say no to others
so I can say YES! to myself.

15

Eliminate Prickly Attitudes

*If you want a place in the sun,
you've got to put up with a few blisters.*
—Abigail Van Buren

What negative thoughts, actions, and reactions do you have when you look at or think about your clutter and debt?

Paula struggled with debt from an early age, on her own as a teenager. By twenty-one, she was dodging collectors, had her car impounded for tickets, and was drinking excessively. Suicide seemed like a viable option. All she was really looking for was a way to ease the pain.

All of us have had a splinter or pricked our finger on a thorn while cutting roses or picking raspberries. Our immediate desire is to ease the pain, so we stick our finger in our mouth to soothe away the prickliness. We do this in many areas of our lives, especially with our attitudes about clutter and debt.

When your clutter and debt overwhelm you, which of the following are your go-to responses to avoid the prickliness of discomfort?

- Buy something to feel better
- Binge-watch television, troll social media, or sleep for hours
- Drink, do drugs, procrasti-bake, or work out excessively
- Search for get-rich-quick business ideas
- Kick the dog, yell at the kids, hit the spouse

When it comes to avoiding the prickliness of debt and clutter, our creativity is endless. As you create an orderly and financially secure life, that prickliness can seem even more pervasive. Just *thinking* about acting on our clutter, paying a bill, or creating a system to help us achieve a goal can trigger us.

It's helpful to remember that the sole goal of prickliness is to derail your forward motion. When you're tempted to put off paying a bill, calling a creditor, organizing, or reducing clutter, pay attention to changes in your attitude. Where are you short-tempered with others (or yourself) because you don't like the way debt or clutter makes you feel?

Before you give yourself permission to avoid a task you want to achieve, have a pep talk with yourself by answering these two questions:

1. What will I gain by getting out of debt?
2. What are my payoffs for getting organized and decluttering?

Earlier, we mentioned roses and raspberries because they're good examples of payoffs that come with discomfort. Let's say you really want to have roses gracing your living room or you want ripe berries for breakfast, but you're not a big fan of being stuck by thorns. So you ask yourself: *Is the prickliness—the minor discomfort—worth it to have what I want?*

Answering this question, you will create ways to reduce or eliminate the prickliness so you can have what you really want. You could choose to wear gloves, get someone else to pick the roses or raspberries, or give the task your undivided, careful attention and minimize the prickliness.

We use roses and raspberries intentionally here. Roses gracing a room represent the open, flowy feeling of a clutter-free home. A bowl of berries represents the abundance you feel when you eliminate a debt, build savings, or achieve a positive net worth.

Today, pick one thing to reorganize or one financial issue to move forward. Make it simple. Ask yourself if there's a single credit card you want to cut up today, or sort through a single pile of clutter to see what is ripe to be tossed, sold, or given away.

Remind yourself of why you want to take the action, what your payoff will be, and become determined to act despite any emotional prickly thorns. Each time you do, you reduce the effect your prickly attitudes have on you. Your benefits will be as satisfying as a good bowl of berries and as pleasing as a fragrant rose.

Affirm

Just for today, I trade in my prickly attitudes for an army of payoffs.

16

Accept (and Ask for) Forgiveness

It's easier to ask forgiveness than it is to get permission.
—Admiral Grace Hopper

Where does debt or clutter control your daily life, draining energy and attention that you could give to yourself or loved ones?

Janet knew a man whose children believed he loved his stuff more than he loved them. He was clueless about their feelings until they confronted him.

It's easy to overlook the effects of our words and actions. The items and debt we accumulate during our lifetime impact us and others. Defending our clutter and debt (consciously or unconsciously) creates disagreement and disharmony. Accepting our role in the conflicts we've created empowers us to change things, to mend fences.

But admitting we're wrong, or that we've contributed to someone else's pain, calls on our courage and humility. This process requires rigorous honesty with yourself. Today, take a fearless emotional inventory of your clutter and debt by asking yourself these seven questions with complete honesty:

1. WHY am I afraid to get rid of things?
2. WHAT do these things represent to me?
3. HOW have my treasures and clutter affected me and my family?
4. WHERE have I spent money on things I decided were *important* to me instead of things that were *necessary* for my family or myself?
5. WHEN did I borrow money from someone and never repay them?
6. WHEN did I borrow items from someone and never returned them or returned them in worse shape?
7. WHERE do I need to make amends and ask for forgiveness?

If something is amiss in a relationship and you'd like to mend it, this inner reflection is the key: willingly make amends, ask for forgiveness, and accept the other person's reaction, whether positive, negative, or neutral.

It's equally important to forgive yourself. Paula teaches clients that self-forgiveness begins with accepting the following statement about all past choices you've made: *it seemed like a good idea at the time.* Which is the truth. If it hadn't seemed like a good idea at the time, you wouldn't have done it!

Past actions *don't* have to affect your future actions. Repeat the following statement if you find yourself wanting to beat yourself up for past choices: *I forgive myself for everything I have ever done—or perceive that I have done—that negatively affected myself or others. I accept my forgiveness and release the past, now.*

Today, choose to deal with your clutter and debt differently. Ask for and accept forgiveness for your past actions, and move forward toward the orderly and financially secure life you desire.

Affirm

Just for today, I accept forgiveness and make amends for my past choices.

17

Release Fear of What Might Happen

Commit yourself to pushing through the fear and becoming more than you are at the present moment.
—Susan Jeffers

What are you most afraid will happen if you do (or don't) conquer your clutter and debt? Worry and fear are learned behaviors, and, luckily, are also easily *unlearned*.

Paula was very excited when, at age thirty, she was about to buy her first home. Three days before closing, her lender called. They couldn't approve her FHA loan because her credit report showed an outstanding balance on a federal student loan that she had paid off years earlier.

Paula worried she'd lose her chance to buy the house of her dreams and had no idea how to fix the error. She paused for a minute to release her fears of what might happen and a simple question came to mind: *how much does it show I still owe, and what's the quickest way to pay it?* The answer: Ninety-three dollars in unpaid interest from when she paid off the loan. And she could hand-deliver payment to a local office. Armed with this information, she took care of the issue over her lunch break.

Information *is* power.

Someone, somewhere, taught us to be afraid, to worry. We learned that we shouldn't throw anything away in case we need it later, that giving away gifts would disappoint the giver, or that creditors are mean and nasty. Someone taught us to be afraid to ask for help. We've even been taught to be afraid of having an orderly and financially secure life.

The best way to move *past* fear is to first gain clarity *about* the fear. To shine a light on the origins of your fears, ask yourself these six questions:

1. WHAT would happen if I threw away or gave away everything I don't find useful or don't absolutely love?
2. WHAT is it about money that scares me?
3. WHAT is the worst that could happen if I threw away every paper that said, "Keep this paper for your records"?

4. WHAT would happen if I paid only what I could truly afford on my debts instead of paying what my creditors demand?
5. WHAT would happen if the process of decluttering made my space messier before it got neater?
6. WHAT would happen if my credit report was less than perfect for a while?

When you're done, review your answers and ask yourself: *am I sure that's what would happen?* Overcoming fear is sometimes as simple as releasing our expectations of what *might* happen. Just because we believe it will happen doesn't make it so!

It is common to fear someone saying no. This fear keeps us from asking for what we want until we are in a state of desperation, where any no answer devastates us.

Today, dissolve this fear, using these four steps:
1. Ask for something you have absolutely no desire to receive. For example, if you hate black licorice or don't smoke, ask people if they have any licorice or a cigarette.
2. Ask for something where you don't care if the other person says yes. Randomly asking for a safety pin, paper clip, or piece of chewing gum is a good option.

3. Ask for help with something you could easily do for yourself, so the other person's answer has no power. Ask for help bringing in a few bags of groceries or handing you something you could easily reach yourself.
4. Ask for help when you truly need assistance. Ask for help organizing an out-of-reach area, hauling away large items, negotiating a lower monthly payment, or setting up a workable payment plan in order to avoid a court judgment.

Lower your fear level, and it's easier to release expectations about the answer you receive. And it becomes acceptable to you that the answer you receive may still be no.

When you speak to creditors with less fear, you'll discover how to talk to them so they listen. Loved ones become more willing to communicate and join your efforts to declutter and reduce debt.

Staying vague about your fears feeds and strengthens them. Quickly conquer your debt by facing fears of what might happen and releasing your attachment to the outcome of events. Each time you face a fear, you reduce its power over you.

Let your courage guide you. Share your feelings and talk through your most pressing issues about clutter and debt. Sharing your fears disarms them so they can no longer paralyze you.

Acknowledge, reframe, and release one fear today, and you'll take a giant step forward in your quest for financial freedom and an orderly life.

Affirm

Just for today, I release my fears about what might happen and embrace the positive possibilities instead.

18

Pause Procrastination

An excuse is a universally accepted lie about why we don't do something we want or ought to do.
—Rick Butts

Where has procrastination affected your ability to move toward the life you really want?

Here is a real-life example from our lives. When Janet left Paula's publishing company to build a personal organizing company, Paula became solely responsible for everything in her publishing company, including triaging emails, which previously had been handled by Janet. An email from Harpo Productions, owned by Oprah Winfrey, sat in Paula's inbox for weeks before she responded to their request for information on her Break the Debt Cycle—for Good! program for an upcoming show.

Paula received a polite response back, thanking her and letting her know that since they hadn't heard from her sooner, they had decided to go with another financial expert. That episode aired a few months later, introducing the world to a then little-known financial planner named Suze Orman. Overwhelmed by email clutter, Paula procrastinated, leading to a missed opportunity to appear on national television.

If you've ever said, *I'll act on that later* or *I'll take care of this financial issue tomorrow*, congratulate yourself: you have already mastered justifying or excusing your procrastination. Woo-hoo!

Luckily, research shows that all you need do to avoid the pesky negative consequences of procrastination is to take one small action at that moment. One effortless way to pause procrastination and reprogram your consciousness is to simply declare, *I'm taking a minute to do this now.* Then do it.

For example, before the days of direct deposit, ATMs, and banking apps, Paula had a client who regularly bounced checks simply because she didn't deposit her paycheck right away. Her excuse? By the time she got off work Friday, the bank was closed. Sometimes her paycheck stayed in her purse for *weeks* before being deposited. Paula suggested she get a night deposit bag from the bank so she could drop her paycheck in the night deposit box on her way home each Friday. Her deposits were then recorded the next business day, breaking the cycle of bounced checks.

When you're tempted to delay action, use Janet's 5 W's for Overcoming Procrastination to uncover your self-sabotage. Ask (and answer) these five questions:

5 W's for Overcoming Procrastination
1. WHY don't I want to do this task?
2. WHAT am I afraid of?
3. WHAT would I rather be doing instead of vaporizing my clutter and debt?
4. WHAT would happen if I accomplished this task?
5. WHAT am I *really* trying to achieve?

Today, instead of stressing over what's still left to do with your clutter and debt, settle down. Let the whirlwind of ideas, thoughts, worries—all the shoulds and shouldn'ts—become still.

In that stillness, declare that you *will* take one action to eliminate fear and build confidence in creating an orderly and financially stable life for yourself. Think through everything you want to accomplish today, and prioritize your list.

Next, imagine you're only able to take three actions today. Which three would have the biggest impact for your life?

Finally, use Janet's 5 W's of Prioritizing to pare your list.

5 W's of Prioritizing

1. WHAT small task have I been avoiding that will help me free up space, time, or cash flow as quickly as possible?
2. WHY do I want to do this task?
3. WHEN does this task have to be done to avoid additional chaos or financial stress? (Look at due dates, renewal dates, dates when additional fees or expenses will be charged, dates when company is coming, when you'll need something for a meeting or an outing.)
4. WHERE will I find the information needed to act?
5. WHAT lasting benefit do I gain from taking this action?

Cut your list until you have three top priorities. Setting priorities helps our brains outline the best path for getting out of our own way. Focus on what is most important to you—creating order and financial stability—and you put a wrench in your ego's maniacal plans for interrupting your progress.

Once you've picked your top three priorities for today, congratulate yourself. Take a deep breath. And then act. One baby step, one proactive choice at a time, toward your three most important tasks will create more order in your life and your finances today.

Invest twenty minutes in yourself and prove you are the strong and steady tortoise, always moving forward toward your heart's desire to be debt-free and clutter-free. Your success is assured today as you act on three small priorities you've been avoiding until now.

Affirm

Just for today, I pause procrastination.

19

Embrace Your Worthiness

Be brave, be curious, be determined,
overcome the odds. It can be done.
—STEPHEN HAWKING

Who told you what you could or could not do in your life? How did their beliefs about you squelch your dreams or motivate you to achieve them?

Paula decided early on she was going to be a writer and told everyone this was her dream job. To which her father responded, "You can't make a living as a writer." Paula's inner response was, *oh, yeah? I'll show you!* Later in life, she realized that her father's statement was her ultimate motivation. She often says that if her father had been outwardly supportive of her desire to write for a living, she probably would have never pursued writing as her career. She would have abandoned herself instead of embracing her worthiness.

Abandonment issues often lead us to abandon ourselves and our dreams. Healing clutter and debt issues begins with recognizing where and how we abandon ourselves. The more we can identify where we abandon ourselves, the better we can understand why we think and act as we do with our money and possessions.

Without judgment, today recognize what you've created in your life. The actions you took (or didn't take) have all contributed to your accumulation of debt and excess belongings. All actions were based on information you had at that moment. Answer these ten questions and give yourself new information to work with:

1. WHERE do I put everyone else before myself?
2. WHY don't I believe I deserve to treat myself with as much love and compassion as I give others?
3. WHY do I keep things that have outlived their usefulness?
4. WHERE have I created a void in my life?
5. WHERE do I look outside myself to fill that void?
6. WHERE do I put other people's comfort before my own?
7. WHERE do I care more about what other people think than about having an orderly and financially secure life?

8. WHERE am I more concerned with keeping up appearances than being debt-free?
9. WHERE do I put my creditors' approval and their agenda ahead of my own family's well-being?
10. WHERE do I run away from people, problems, situations, and gifts—including myself?

We learned every belief we have before we were seven years old, back when our brains were sponges. Replace these unconsciously learned lessons with beliefs that align with self-love. Fill your heart with love, and respond to your heart's desires rather than the voices of lack, limitation, and fear. Uncovering these fears and deep-seated roots will help you create an orderly and financially stable life.

Remember: you are *always* at choice. You can believe someone else's value of yourself. Or you can recognize why you do what you do, release beliefs that don't serve you anymore, and embrace your true worthiness. It's time for you to soar.

Affirm
Just for today, I allow my soul to feel its worth.

20

Accept More Simplicity and Abundance

*[Living simply] is a way to create lives filled with peace
and fulfillment for ourselves and for others.*
—Linda Breen Pierce

What would it look and feel like to simplify your life? How can you create both simplicity *and* abundance? Where do you feel you would have to sacrifice one or the other?

When Paula's family downsized from a 4,000-square-foot, six-bedroom, four-bath home to an 1,100-square-foot, three-bedroom, one-bath home, the benefits exceeded expectations. A huge reduction in possessions, utility bills, and other household expenses was a given. The unexpected, but most valuable, benefit was that their teenage son now spends more time hanging out in the living room, engaging in deep conversations, doing his homework, playing video games, and sharing his life with his parents.

The move created both simplicity and abundance in both tangible and intangible ways. But what exactly *are* simplicity and abundance?

Everyone has their own idea of what constitutes a simple life. To some, it is heading to work, coming home, spending the evening with family or friends, going to bed, and repeating the process the next day. To others, a simple life eliminates the chaos, the frantic pace, the everyday clutter and overwhelm. To still others, a simple life is getting back to basics, paring down expenses, eliminating packaged products, and creating a more organized and organic life.

Likewise, everyone has their own idea of what constitutes an abundant life. To some, abundance is having more money, time, or experiences. To others, it means having more peace of mind and less worry. To still others, abundance means living a life that's fully aligned with their values: a fully authentic life.

Sometimes your desires for simplicity and abundance may seem contradictory. Explore and clarify your beliefs about these questions with these three steps:

1. Sit down and determine exactly what having more simplicity and abundance in your life would mean to you and your family and what that new life could look like.

2. Brainstorm and write down all actions that could bring you closer to your dream for simplicity and abundance.
3. List all hesitations that pop up to drown your dream of welcoming simplicity and authentic abundance into your life.

We often spend our time and energy *rejecting* clutter and debt. Today, invest energy in *accepting* the simplicity and abundance you crave. Do the above exercise with rigorous honesty, and you'll begin seeing what you truly want. You'll discover how to make your orderly life a reality.

Increase your willingness to accept what *is* right now and use your notes from the above exercise to move you toward the specific simplicity and abundance you've outlined. Believe that it *is* possible to have what you desire. Then look for opportunities to create what you desire, today, despite any apparent contradiction.

Affirm

*Just for today, I accept more simplicity
and abundance in my life.*

21

Appreciate Your Current View

Contentment is not a bank balance, marital status, or pot of gold you reach at the end of the rainbow. It is a choice you make, an attitude you step into, a state of being that runs deeper than conditions.

—ALAN COHEN

Why are you unhappy with the current level of order and financial security in your life? When will you *know* you've reached a level of contentment with both?

On our Enough Is Enough! tours, we started each event by sharing how the concept of *enough* is an illusion. The word means *sufficient* or *satisfactory*. And those meanings differ depending on the context.

Imagine two situations where the noise is at the same loud level. One situation is at a concert you're fully enjoying. The other situation involves people arguing, and the noise makes you want to shout, *that's enough!* The noise level is the same in terms of decibels, but one is acceptable and the other is not.

We sort clutter and debt into similar levels: those that are normal, tolerable, or unacceptable *to us*. Today, analyze your current perception of your clutter and debt by answering these two questions:

1. *What do I consider clutter?* Is it unused items taking up space, being unable to open a closet or cabinet without something falling out on me, or being unable to find things when I want them?
2. *What do I consider debt?* Is it carrying a balance on credit cards, the inability to pay anything on outstanding bills, or unexpected events that require me to tap my savings or use credit?

Your perception of clutter and debt may keep you focused on the negative. You know the drill: We look at our collections or accumulated piles and berate ourselves for the chaos and disorder, or for the money spent. We glare at outstanding balances and chastise ourselves for what we must postpone because our income is tied up paying for things bought with credit. Judging our clutter and debt keeps us from seeing the beauty around us.

Today, refresh your view by bringing your thoughts into the present. Once upon a time, every bit of clutter and every penny of debt was something you desired, although you now look upon it with disdain.

Today, release the desire to fix or escape from your clutter and debt. Release the past and all its judgments, and take time to appreciate and enjoy where you are today.

Look at your clutter and your bills with eyes of appreciation. Don't focus on what sidetracked your quest to reduce clutter and debt. Instead, take time to appreciate what you behold. Maybe you've created the biggest, best mess of your finances and your living space. Appreciate your accomplishment. If you could accomplish creating all this clutter and debt, imagine the amazing way you will accomplish creating order and financial security!

Today, take time to appreciate your life from this new viewpoint. Yes, you may have piles of bills and an abundance of items in your home, but that doesn't mean they're burdens. Sit quietly and remember what joy you experienced when you purchased everything in your life and all the benefits your bills represent. Recognize and congratulate yourself—in a judgment-free way—on the progress you've made. Just for today, be content with that progress.

Affirm

Just for today, I appreciate what I see in my life, and celebrate my progress.

22

Know Perfect Harmony Is Your Life

The mind has a powerful way of attracting things that are in harmony with it, good and bad.
—Idowu Koyenikan

Where in your life do you feel out of balance or out of harmony with who you really are? Where does your ego like to blame other people for that imbalance and disharmony?

Janet experienced this sense of imbalance decades ago, with her husband. At the end of the workday, Janet unwound by making dinner for them, often before she went out to speak at an evening event. A few nights a week, her husband would unwind with colleagues at a local tavern after work, and sometimes he forgot to tell Janet he'd be home late. Janet would get angry at him—

until she realized she was actually mad at *herself* and decided to get back in harmony with herself.

She began making dinner for herself each night and enjoyed leisurely preparing for her evening out, regardless of what her hubby did. He could pick and choose from leftovers as he desired, and he quickly realized the key to having a hot meal and dinner with his wife was to let her know his plans by early afternoon. Janet created a lighthearted solution that empowered them both.

Our lives are naturally filled with light and laughter. Our egos, however, like focusing on what's dull and gloomy—those places where we feel out of balance.

We use the word *feel* deliberately here. Your life isn't actually out of balance: it only feels that way because you're out of balance with your own natural rhythm and harmony.

Make a list of everything you feel is out of harmony with your true self. All those outer influences: relationship issues, conflicts, addictions, compulsions, health or weight challenges, unexpected illnesses or deaths, interruptions in income, past due bills, computer crashes, appliance repairs, misfiled papers, embarrassing levels of clutter. Whatever it is for you. Observe where some items have a bigger emotional charge than others.

In *Hamlet*, Shakespeare wrote, "There is nothing either good or bad, but thinking makes it so." Every situation draws power from our perception. We see situations rocking our boat when we just want to float through life on Serenity Bay.

A situation is either dark or light depending on how *you* view it. The song "That's What My Heart's Telling Me" captures this perfectly in the line, "One woman smiles 'cause the sun is shining, same day, another woman's praying for rain."

Everything in our lives is like a piano, with both light and dark keys. If you hit just the ivory keys or just the ebony ones, the music created won't be nearly as rich as what you create when you let the light and dark work together. This is the rhythmic, balanced interchange showing us that everything in nature works together in harmony.

An avid bird whisperer, Janet spent hours in her backyard each day, observing and interacting with her feathered friends. Watching mockingbirds build large, elaborate nests every year fascinated her. If their nest was destroyed, the mockingbird simply rebuilt somewhere else, allowing other birds to salvage twigs to build their own nests. The process flowed in perfect harmony, with no sense of loss or despair.

As you create order and financial security, stuff is going to happen. You're making progress, paying off debts, getting financially organized, releasing clutter, creating order. Then something you come across triggers a sad, angry, or depressing memory and completely derails you. You shut down, throw your hands up and declare, *I can't do this*! If this happens today, take a step back and take a deep breath (or ten).

It's not our memory that shuts us down; it's our thoughts about what those memories *mean* about our clutter and debt and by extension *us*. Pause what you're doing when something you come across knocks your nest out of the tree. Recognize the meaning that you're giving to the memory. And remember the perfect harmony that's within you.

Give yourself permission to feel your feelings, and then change your perception by looking for the blessing in the memory, using these four tools:

1. Train your thoughts to stay present and in perfect harmony with the world around you today.
2. Act *as if* every area of your life were in perfect harmony. Learn to recognize when you perceive something dark in your life.
3. Look for ways to blend the light with the dark.
4. Take a deep breath and focus on the adjustments you can make in your thoughts to recognize the harmony and balance in your life.

Affirm

Just for today, I see myself knowing that perfect harmony is the guiding light in my life.

23

Acknowledge Your True Value

Before you can win, you have to believe you are worthy.
—Mike Ditka

What is your payoff for thinking you are unworthy? What do you *gain* by believing you're unworthy, and what are you afraid you will *lose* if you acknowledge your true value?

When Paula was a child, she stuttered. She rarely spoke, and when she did, she spoke quietly and as quickly as she could, since someone else was bound to finish her sentences for her. She valued avoiding ridicule more than she valued what she had to say.

This may sound harsh, but it's true: valuing someone or something more than you value yourself creates a mental block to knowing your own true value. Devaluing yourself is the highest form of self-destruction.

Instead of giving value to your clutter and debt, let's begin to dissolve that block by acknowledging and claiming the value you place on creating an orderly, financially secure life. Both values exist within you, like two sides of a teeter-totter. Part of us wants to move forward with creating order out of chaos. Yet we also feel guilty or fearful about what these positive changes will mean about us and what our new life will look like.

We knew a woman who trimmed her weight down by more than 100 pounds. She suddenly found herself flocked by suitors and made some relationship choices she regretted. She stated, "My body went where my brain wasn't ready to go." Her brain still saw herself as overweight and unattractive; it wasn't ready to handle her revealed beauty.

Finding balance between our different levels of self-value often leads to self-sabotage. We sabotage our efforts to get clutter-free or debt-free because a part of us doesn't really believe we *are* orderly or financially secure, or even that we deserve to be. We think we *should* be, but we don't think we are.

Today, silence all other shoulds except for one: you *should* be living a life that is true to yourself. Which often means leaving chunks of your current life and beliefs behind. Today, focus on what you *are* instead of what you are not.

Valuing yourself may seem difficult. It's not; it's just different to do something you think you cannot do. Identify your internal blocks and embrace this different way of thinking by answering these two questions:

1. WHAT part of my clutter have I most hoped would go away by itself?
2. WHAT financial change have I avoided making because of what others might say or think?

Today, value yourself enough to act on the most daunting part of your clutter. Value yourself enough to make one financial change for yourself, regardless of how others may react. When fear appears, remind yourself that you *are* worthy of living in an organized, financially stable world today.

Empower yourself even more and acknowledge the positive things you value by answering these questions:

1. WHAT have I been yearning for?
2. WHO do I know who lives in that desired world more than I do?
3. WHO has reached the financial contentment I want to achieve?
4. WHO has created the balance and order I crave?

Allow yourself to acknowledge you are worthy of having the same in your life.

Affirm

Just for today, I fully value having an organized, financially stable life.

24

Take Nourishment from Everyone and Everything

We are rich only through what we give,
and poor only through what we refuse.
—Anne Sophie Swetchine

Where do you allow your friends and loved ones to nourish you with unbridled enthusiasm, and where do you dampen their spirits? Where do you act on their enthusiasm and accept their assistance, and where do you make excuses for why now is not a good time? Where do you see people being a help and where do you see them being a nuisance?

Both of us can relate to this "all by myself or not at all" mindset; we both were on our own at an early age. Although this belief served us well in some areas, it was a detriment in other areas—until we both learned the value of being nourished by others.

Nourishment comes in many forms, some even more vital to us than food. Abandoned babies in a hospital are fed, yet they will die if they're not picked up and held. Sometimes we nourish our pets more than ourselves. We groom and pet and fuss over them. We allow our pets to shower us with unbridled passion and enthusiasm and never dampen their spirits. Yet we often don't do that with other people—or ourselves.

We refuse to let others nourish us because we don't feel we deserve to be nourished. We feel we should be able to nourish ourselves, yet we often don't. We feel ashamed, embarrassed, too proud to accept help or even compliments.

Today, when someone compliments you on the progress you've made toward reducing your debt and clutter, allow that compliment to sink in and feed you. Take nourishment from the progress you've made by acknowledging what you've already accomplished rather than what remains on your to-do list.

For example, when you take your next right action to clean up a financial area or reduce a bill, pause a moment and look at what you've already accomplished. Give yourself credit (no pun intended) for the systems you've already created. Look at the amount you've already paid. Celebrate your progress before giving attention to the remaining balance, new charges, or whatever financial step is next your list.

When you walk into a room, look first at what you've already cleared out and organized. Celebrate the space you've opened up before you give any attention to piles or tasks that still remain.

The peril of doing everything all by yourself is that sometimes we don't know what we don't know. What tasks have you been avoiding because you don't know the next best step? Maybe you don't know what papers you need to keep or for how long, or what to do with a specific item. Or you're stuck trying to figure out a system to create order out of your chaos.

When Paula was asked to put together a fifteen-year anniversary edition of her classic book *The Art of Tithing* (formerly *Giving Thanks*), she wanted to make the study guide easier to use. No matter how she looked at it, she couldn't seem to figure out a clear and simple system. Stuck, she got quiet, and asked herself, *who would know how to do this?* One person immediately popped into her mind: a literary agent and writing coach whose class she'd attended a year earlier. She immediately emailed the woman, outlining the issue and explaining her desire to hire the coach for her expertise. Within a few days, the coach provided a simple solution, which made the study guide flow with grace.

When you feel stuck today, get quiet and ask, *who would know how to do this?*

People aren't mind readers, *and* they do want to help. Even if no one pops into your mind while you're quiet, you've sent your request out to the universe. Your job is to pay attention to the universe's answers. Listen when someone offers advice or assistance that would apply to your situation. You don't necessarily have to act on the advice: it may be a gateway to the information you seek. Or it may contain a kernel of hard truth you need to hear or gentle nourishment that affirms you're on the right track. If discouragement or fear comes up, ask clarifying questions until the simple solution unfolds itself.

Today, recognize that everyone has some sort of nourishment for you, and accept that nourishment. Don't withhold from yourself. Give yourself permission to accept their nourishment and to nourish yourself as well.

Affirm

*Just for today, I nourish myself and accept
the nourishment others have for me.*

25

Approach Life with Open Arms

The purpose of life, after all, is to live it,
to taste experience to the utmost, to reach out eagerly
and without fear for newer and richer experience.
—Eleanor Roosevelt

How do you feel when you watch a child play with wild abandon?

Every summer, Paula's young friend AndreaRose walked to the park near her home in Cocoa Village, Florida, on the day the park turned on its water fountain. She stood in the middle, fully clothed, arms open wide, head thrown back, her body lit up with outrageous laughter; no care about wet clothes or what someone might say.

After AndreaRose passed away at the tender age of nine, many people mentioned at her memorial service how they had often thought about jumping into the fountain fully clothed, but never had. That summer, when the water fountain turned on, countless adults were there, jumping in fully clothed to honor AndreaRose's zest for life.

Today, approach your desire for an organized and financially secure life with this same wild abandon. Instead of getting defensive about your progress with clutter and debt, think and speak with love, joy, and acceptance.

Imagine releasing your inner limitations, criticisms, and fears. Celebrate the wondrous changes you've created toward order and financial security. Notice your unexpected smile as you release worry about bill collectors calling or visitors seeing your clutter. Forget about *how* you're going to finish getting rid of all your clutter and debt, and stay in the moment.

The simple act of *doing something in this moment* toward order and financial security will bring you what you desire. Every pile you sort, every drawer you organize, every item you give away, toss, or file brings you closer to your goal. Every creditor you call, every dollar of debt you pay off, every choice you make about how to spend or not spend your resources does the same.

Today, seek and find the fun in clearing clutter and eliminating debt. Enjoy the treasure hunt of sorting, where every pile potentially contains an unexpected treasure, and of paying bills, where every dollar paid on a debt brings you closer to personal wealth.

Experience the feeling of joy that comes with each action, the feeling of being ready, willing, and able to enjoy whatever comes into your life as you build the orderly, financially secure life you desire.

Affirm

Just for today, I approach my clutter and debt
with open arms and wild abandon.

26

Call on Your Inner Power

This too shall pass.
—Persian adage

When you feel overwhelmed with clutter and debt, how do you react? Do you shut down, speed up, throw in the towel, try to force a solution, rage against yourself or the world, or something else?

Paula once worked with a church that was experiencing some chaos. At one meeting, when board members were rushing around trying to force a specific solution to an emerging problem, Paula calmly asked if they wanted to pause and pray. One person blurted out, "We don't have *time* to pray!"

Ever have one of those days?

Our efforts to create order and financial security can sometimes dig us in deeper. We think we're fixing one problem, but it turns out we're creating another.

When you start creating order, things may get messier for a bit. Sometimes the process feels like walking in quicksand: the more we struggle, the deeper we sink. Overwhelm takes control of our brains, and we switch into fight, flight, or freeze mode, derailing our efforts.

The axiom "This too shall pass" is true. Everything comes and goes. Your job is to bring yourself back to a calm, cool, collected state of mind so you can continue your mission of creating the life you truly desire.

Navy SEALs have a saying: "Slow is smooth; smooth is fast." When you slow down, things move more smoothly. When things move smoothly, your goals get accomplished faster. If you ever catch fire, you're not supposed to run around like a maniac. You're supposed to stop, drop, and roll.

When you have an emergency, you call 911. You tell the operator the problem and request the help you need: a fire truck, ambulance, the police. The operator tells you to stay on the line and gives you instructions to help stabilize the situation, assuring you that help is on the way. Your 911 call is a way of connecting with a power greater than yourself.

Today, when you reach a stuck place, connect with your Inner Power. Get quiet and ask for assistance and instructions for moving forward. It doesn't matter what you call that Inner Power—God, Higher Power, or Jiminy Cricket (which is what Paula called hers for years). All that matters is getting into the habit of turning within for clarity about what's yours to do when you're at your wits' end.

Tell your Inner Power exactly what you need. Then grow quiet, listen to the specific instructions your Inner Power gives you, and follow the guidance you receive.

Affirm

*Just for today, I connect with my
Inner Power for guidance.*

27

Nurture Your Discomfort Zone

*People remain in their comfort zone in order to avoid pain,
but it eventually keeps them from fully living.*
—Phil Stutz and Barry Michels

When you are making progress toward creating order and financial security, where do you find yourself tempted to take on new chaos, clutter, expenses, or debt?

Many experts define the comfort zone as a place that makes us feel safe and secure, without anxiety. The truth is, what most of us view as our comfort zone is really just our "familiar zone."

Changing what's familiar to us—making progress toward order and financial security—moves us into unfamiliar territory. It moves us out of our comfort zone. Subconsciously, we seek ways to get back to the familiar, but that can lead us back into clutter and debt. And we usually don't even realize what we're doing!

When Janet and her husband received an inheritance, they immediately used the funds to pay off debt and do home improvements. Before they knew it, the inheritance was spent, and they were back to the same level of debt as before.

Today, pay attention when you're tempted to purchase something on credit again, spend money you've freed up in your budget, or fill newly organized areas with new clutter. Examine what drives the impulse to return to your comfortable level of chaos and financial scarcity. Examine where you want to "reward" yourself for your hard work by basically undoing your progress. The sooner you identify this subconscious pull, the easier it will be to break the cycle.

Today, reframe the reward you're creating for yourself. Your reward is the order and financial security you desire, and the creation of a lifestyle that supports and sustains that order and security. Acknowledge all the ways your clutter-free space creates openness in your life. Celebrate when you make purchases without taking on new debt, and all the other ways your freed resources can grow your net worth.

Alcoholics Anonymous has a slogan: "Think through the drink." Meaning, before you decide to take that all too familiar drink, run a movie through your mind showing how the story will end. Usually it's not what anyone trying to stay sober from clutter or debt wants to create.

Today, think through the familiarity of your clutter and debt, visualize where it has led you in the past, choose to embrace your discomfort zone, and take action to change your story's ending.

Affirm
Just for today, I boldly step into my discomfort zone.

28

Forgive All Past Decisions

It seemed like a good idea at the time.
—Source unknown

What false beliefs are you holding on to because of what someone in your past did or said?

Paula had a hard time saving money for many years until she finally realized why. As a young child, she was a master saver, socking away almost everything that came her way. Whenever her family's financial situation got tight, however, her father would borrow from her piggy bank. He always left her small paper chits saying "I owe you," but the money was never repaid. Subconsciously, she incorporated a belief that if she saved money, someone else would take it from her. So it became easier to *not* save money.

A clutter-bound client once told Janet, "My mother taught me well. I cannot let go of anything."

The key to self-forgiveness is remembering that no matter what was said or done, it truly did seem like a good idea at the time. If it hadn't, it wouldn't have happened.

It's time to shed beliefs that hold you back. Today, forgive someone who taught you inappropriate habits about money or possessions, who taught you how to hoard or didn't teach you how to budget your money. Forgive yourself for taking on their belief; for overspending and for using items to fill an emotional need.

Paula's belief about building savings remained stuck in the past until she decided to take control of her financial life and believe in her ability to save rather than believing that anyone else's choices had power over her finances. She forgave her father and herself for perpetuating her mistaken financial belief.

Extending forgiveness today is vital to gaining freedom from clutter and debt. What happened in the past belongs in the past.

Every moment you spend reliving hurts and false beliefs from your past distracts your attention from the good in your life—and the greater good coming to you today.

How do you forgive someone? Recall the story you tell yourself about the person and what you believe they did. With that story in mind, see them as having done the best they could do and declare:

Forgive All Past Decisions

It seemed like a good idea at the time. I know you did the best you could do at the time. And now it's time for me to take control of my life and let go of beliefs that no longer serve me. You taught me well, but you taught me wrong. I now give myself permission to change my beliefs.

Do your forgiveness work while looking at a picture of the person, or offer your declaration of release to the universe.

Make a list of all past hurts and beliefs that currently influence your life. Release them—heck, burn the paper you've written them on if you want. Then quietly reflect on what you truly want in your life. Financial peace, organized space, time to simply relax and breathe instead of struggling. Write your desires down and install them like software into the space created by your choices to heal, forgive, and release all past decisions—yours and others'.

Affirm

Just for today, I forgive myself for every decision I've made, knowing it was a good idea at the time.

29

Adopt a Positive Attitude

If you're at the end of your rope...
untie the knot in your heart.
—Cooper Edens

When you have zero interest in dealing with your clutter or paying attention to your finances, to what outside forces or inner beliefs are you giving your power?

Janet had a client who firmly believed he couldn't clean up his clutter because items out of sight were items out of mind. Paula had a client who was afraid to pay bills (and often incurred late fees) because her spouse once mentioned they should always have at least $1,000 in their checking account.

Our daily attitudes about clutter and debt are swayed by many things. Not enough time, sleep, or energy. Nothing to wear, lack of knowledge, or feeling completely overwhelmed. The weather, our health, other people's beliefs, or their milquetoast commitment to *our* goals.

Negative attitudes creep up on us when we aren't taking good care of ourselves, when we resent someone, fear something, believe we lack knowledge or skills, or are trying to do something that simply isn't ours to do at that moment. We transfer our negative attitudes to the goals we've set for creating order and financial stability. We see our own goals as impossible: dreadful chores rather than cherished outcomes. Our negative attitude creates a downward emotional spiral.

Giving yourself a time-out—taking time to shift to a positive attitude—can just as easily uplift you and open new creative solutions. Feel the aha! moment that emanates from your time-out and empowers you to move forward toward your orderly and financially stable life.

The man who dreaded organizing realized he could create an organized *visible* place for everything. Rather than seeing organizing as a hide-and-seek venture, he organized things where he could easily see and find them and just as easily return them to where they belonged.

The woman who felt stuck financially realized she didn't have to keep the checkbook balance that high as long as she knew what was scheduled to come into and out of the account on a daily basis. Armed with this knowledge, she chose to have a lower checkbook balance, pay all bills when they were due, and avoid the expense of late fees.

Today, create an "attitude elevation strategy" and activate it whenever a negative attitude becomes persistent. What do you think you *have to* do today? Start by replacing *I have to* with *I get to*, *I choose to*, or our favorite, *I am free to*. Remind yourself: *this too will pass.*

Affirm

Just for today, I gift myself with the freedom to adopt a positive attitude.

30

See Mountains as Speed Bumps

The difference between a mountain and a molehill is your perspective.
—AL NEUHARTH

What makes you think your clutter and debt are huge, unending, insurmountable obstacles to an orderly and financially stable life?

An avid gardener, Janet once ordered half a load of mulch but received an entire load. Instead of a molehill, she came home to four piles of mulch, each over five feet high. Taller than Janet. She went to work on the piles with the best of intentions. She moved mountains of mulch all by herself for hours, mulching every evening until she couldn't mulch anymore. After a few days, her body told her she was done. She realized she needed help, so she hired someone to move the mulch for her.

We all have financial issues and clutter of some sort. Whether you see your clutter and debt as immovable mountains or mere speed bumps in your path to an orderly and financially stable life is up to you.

As an organizer, Janet's visits to see friends were often greeted with an apology for their home being in "such a mess." To which she'd simply respond, "I'm here to visit you, not your house." She didn't see the mess because she was there for the friendship.

Today, practice seeing your clutter and debt as manageable, conquerable, and under control. All it takes is three simple steps to create this changed attitude: acceptance, willingness, and the ability to divide and conquer.

Step 1. **Accept that you are creating order and financial stability in your life.** Acknowledge every bit of progress you make. In the 1920s, the French psychologist Émile Coué made optimistic autosuggestion very popular with his saying, "Every day, in every way, I am getting better and better." We have adapted Coué's affirmation to fit your goals. Repeat the following throughout the day, and especially whenever you're tempted to judge your situation: *Every day, in every way, my life is more orderly and financially stable.*

Step 2. **Be willing to seek help if you need it.** If you get stuck in your progress and need backup, call in help for a specific place you're stuck. You don't have to hire a professional organizer or financial expert. You could simply phone a friend. When Janet called Paula to share news about her liver cancer and her desire to put her affairs in order before she started treatment, Paula drove across the country to help her.

When Paula arrived, she discovered Janet had been sick for some time and her once very orderly home was in disarray. They spent a week together organizing Janet's home, finances, and final wishes, filling their quality time together with laughter, tears, and decades of memories.

Step 3. **Divide and conquer when you're feeling stuck.** Paula is a consummate overachiever, armed with a bazillion tasks on Todoist (an app for organizing). On days when her schedule overwhelms her, she finds herself doing what she calls the "basketball pivot." Standing with one leg firmly in place, her body moves around in a circle, not knowing which way she wants to go or which decision or task she wants to deal with next. Her solution is to freeze, take a deep breath, and break down the desired outcome into small, discrete tasks. Instead of "laundry," she'll list each step out such as "wash darks, dry darks, fold clothes, put away clothes."

Today, do the same for your clutter and debt. Pick *one* piece of clutter to act on. Take $1 and pay it toward a debt, put it into savings today, or choose not to spend it. That's forward motion. That's fulfilling your statement that every day your life *is* more orderly and financially stable.

Climbing the mountain, reaching the peak of an orderly and financially secure life, is a process. When you look too long at the big picture, you're apt to miss the progress you're actually making.

Today, spend twenty minutes expanding your acceptance, exploring your willingness and envisioning ways to divide and conquer the speed bumps.

Affirm

*Just for today, I focus on transforming
my mountains into speed bumps.*

Lather, Rinse, Repeat

One last thought before we go. We've long admired this advice from the late motivational expert Earl Nightingale: "Never give up on a dream just because of the time it will take to accomplish it. The time will pass anyway." Or as the fish Dory put it in the animated motivational classic *Finding Nemo*, "Just keep swimming."

Go through these pages again and again, as you're guided. Do deep dives on any particular chapter you want to revisit. Practice swimming in your newfound confidence and clarity. Keep unfolding your dream. Boldly transform your mind until nothing stands between you and the orderly, financially secure life you desire.

Adopt a positive attitude. Be persistent. And release your attachment to the outcome.

You've got this.

And if you want some of our nuts-and-bolts tips, techniques, and strategies for giving your clutter and debt an old-fashioned thrashing, visit clutteranddebt.com.

The TEASER

When you get ready to sort through your piles, drawers, closets, cupboards, car, boxes of stuff, and anything else that needs to be sorted through, use the TEASER to help you determine what action you need to take on each article.

Get a garbage can or bag, 10 boxes (or you can make 10 piles with labels) and label them with the following:

Toss it
It's not yours, you don't know who it belongs to, it's outdated, it can't be repaired, you don't need it.

End it
You don't want it, you want to cancel it, or you don't read it.

Act on it
Needs an action, such as your signature, phone call, or immediate attention.

Store it
This will have three boxes: **Current Stuff**, **Things I Need to Reference**, and **Historical Stuff**.

Enter it
Information you need to enter into your planner, calendar, or computer.

Refer/Recycle/Read/Repair
It belongs to someone else, or you think they need it.
Use it again or put into a recycling bin.
Something you want or need to read.
Something that can be fixed.

Be ruthless, determined, and honest and sort *all* your stuff using the TEASER.
    Finally, schedule a date and time to act on items you sorted.

DebtBuster Strategy®

Putting the Debt Buster Strategy to Work for You!

See the chart on the next page. List of all your outstanding debts, their balances, and the interest rates they charge under columns A, B, and C. Divide the amount you owe by 12. Write down that amount on your list under column D. Next, write down the amount of your monthly finance charge under column E. Add your principal payment and your monthly interest together, and enter this amount in column F. This is the amount you need to pay every month to pay your debt in full in one year.

For example, say your balance on your first debt is $1,200. Divided by 12, your principal payment would be $100. If you're paying 20 percent interest, you're paying a $20 finance charge every month. Your combined monthly payment (principal and finance charge) would then be $120 if you want to pay off your card in one year.

A	B	C	D
Debt owed to:	Balance remaining	Interest rate	1/12th principal
1. ABC Credit Card	$1,200	20%; $240/year	$100
2.			
3.			
4.			
5.			
6.			
7.			
8.			
9.			
10.			

Need More Time to Pay Down Your Debts?

Don't worry if you can't pay these amounts all at once. That's where the last two columns of the DebtBuster Strategy comes into play. You can start to pay down your balances by paying the minimum monthly payments listed on your bills, plus the interest that was added to this month's bill. Add up these amounts and enter the total in column G.

E	F	G	H
Monthly Interest	1 year Monthly Payment	Required + interest	Required payment
$20	$120	$50	$30

Still too much to pay? Start smaller by just paying the minimum monthly payment, which you can enter into column H.

SuperDebtBuster Strategy®

Do you have only a set amount, like $50, that you can put toward your existing unsecured debts? Not to worry!

Use the SuperDebtBuster Strategy!

See chart on the next page. List of all your outstanding unsecured debts, their balances, and the total unsecured debts that you owe *everyone* under Columns A, B, and C, even people you haven't been able to pay back in years.

Next, divide the amount you owe on the individual debt by the amount you owe on all your debts. This will tell you the percentage of your total debt that is represented by the individual debt. Write down this percentage on your list under column D. Under column E, write down the total amount you can pay toward all your debts each month. Finally, to calculate how much to pay on this

A	B	C
Debt owed to:	Balance remaining	Total debts owed by me
1. ABC Credit Card	$1,200	$15,000
2.		
3.		
4.		
5.		
6.		
7.		
8.		
9.		
10.		

debt, multiply your total monthly payment (column E) by the percentage you can pay (column D). Write the result in column F to see how much you can pay on this debt each month.

For example, say your balance on your first debt is $1,200, and your total debts equal $15,000. Divide $1,200 by $15,000 and you get 8 percent (0.08). In our example, you can only pay $50 toward all your debts each month. Multiply $50 by 0.08 and you get $4. You can pay $4

D	E	F
Percentage this debt is	Total I can pay monthly	Monthly payment for this debt
8% (0.08)	$50	$4

toward this debt each month. Before you panic and say, "That's not nearly enough! My creditor will never go for that!" keep this in mind: you are treating *all* your creditors equally and fairly. No creditor is getting more than his or her fair share under this plan. This is a plan you can stick with. This plan will keep you sane and keep you steadily paying off your debts. After all, who won the race, the tortoise or the hare? Remember: slow and steady wins the game, every time!

Acknowledgments

This book was made possible through a generous grant from God, who provided us with the inspirational scenery that birthed this book along Arizona Highway 17 one hot July morn.

Our thanks to Rev. Judith McClure for her gracious hospitality. Our gratitude is also due to:

The multitude of subscribers and clients who allowed us into their homes and minds, willingly implemented our strategies, openly shared their stories, and provided essential feedback.

Robbie Hall, for his laid-back response to our commandeering the entire house and generally ignoring him during our writing process, and for his unwavering support of Janet's work.

Sandy Haynes and Cooper Haynes-Ebert, for encouraging Paula's dream.

Richard Smoley, for his attention to detail, and radical inspiration. The supportive team at G&D Media, especially Gilles E. Dana, Evan Litzenblatt, and Ellen Goldberg. David S. Reinhardt of Pyrographx, and Meghan Day Healey of Story Horse, LLC.

And the incomparable Willie Nelson for recording our inspirational theme song, "On the Road Again."

About the Authors

PAULA LANGGUTH RYAN is on a quest to help people understand the power of clear, compassionate communication. Widely recognized for her work as a debt negotiator, mediator, and international conflict resolution consultant, Paula hosted the national daily radio show *Conflict Free Zone* and is author of the financial classic *Bounce Back From Bankruptcy* as well as *The Art of Tithing* and *Manifest the Perfect Mate*. Her *Ryan's Rules of Order* is used as a benchmark guideline for creating sustainaʰ positive outcomes in a multitude of diverse settinɼ

Paula's extraordinary skills at reframing ᴄ cations, and her ability to develop win-win-᠎ without compromise, garner high prᴇ᠎ across industries, organizations, anᵛ and her work have been featureᵛ print, radio, and television outlets.

Paula and her family divide their time between Colorado and New Mexico. Her website: paulalangguthryan.com.

JANET L. HALL's successful organizing and time management techniques used psychology to figure out what motivates people to get and stay organized. She offered customized efficiency strategies for individuals, families, and groups worldwide for twenty-five years until her death in June 2021.

Janet's contributions to the field as a consultant and speaker were recognized by groups such as Federally Employed Women and the Federation of Business and Professional Women. Her unique approach spanned many disciplines of ancient wisdom, modern research, and intuition as she helped individuals, families, and corporations most efficiently use and relate to their spaces, creating the positive change in their lives and their environment that they dreamt about.

www.ingramcontent.com/pod-product-compliance
Lightning Source LLC
Chambersburg PA
CBHW072200070526
44585CB00015B/1237